THE ROLLING STOP...

San Juan County, NM Arrests & Bookings

5h · 🌐

Sherrie Ann Chenault was booked into the San Juan County Detention Center on 1/10/2024 2:27 PM by an unknown law enfor... See more

sanjuancountynm.publicjailrecords.com

Sherrie Ann Chenault | San Juan County, NM Arrests

 20

15 comments · 1 share

YOU'RE IN JAIL, NOW WHAT?

A TIME TO REFLECT AND A TIME TO
LEARN.

WHOEVER LOVES DISCIPLINE LOVES
KNOWLEDGE, BUT WHOEVER HATES
CORRECTION IS STUPID.
PROVERBS 12:1

IN ALL THINGS FIND THE GOOD.
GRATEFUL TO HAVE LEARNED WHAT I
HAD NEGLECTED.

In the crisp chill of the first week of 2024, my life came to an abrupt halt in Farmington, New Mexico. It was a day that started like any other, but a seemingly inconspicuous event triggered a chain of events that would unravel my sense of security.

Absorbed in my thoughts, apparently, I rolled through a flashing red light, unaware that this simple act would lead to a nightmarish sequence. Blue and red lights flickered behind me a few blocks from the incident as a team of police officers pulled me over. A routine traffic stop turned into a cascade of misfortune when an outstanding warrant surfaced for my arresta warrant for a failure to appear in court on a dog at large ticket.

Handcuffed and bewildered, I watched my car being towed away, realizing the gravity of the situation. The warrant had been mailed to an old address, and I had never received the notice at my new residence. A simple oversight int h bureaucratic system had led to me spending a very long night in jail.

The jail itself was a cold, unforgiving cement room with two long tables in the middle. Metal bunks lined the walls of a walk-in- closet-sized room within the larder space. I plead for access to a book or a Bible, yet it fell on deaf ears, adding to my sense of isolation.

The only source of entertainment was a small TV that played reruns of "Law and Order" on a loop as the veteran residence respectfully had complete control of what played on the TV. The conditions were deplorable- a shower with a broken curtain made for full exposer to anyone who decided to clean themselves. A girl was left in soiled pants during her period without any clean alternatives despite requesting some several hours prior, and overall, a jail with an atmosphere of neglect.

In the midst of the terror, I experienced a transformative realization. I understand that everything happened for a reason, and even in the darkest moments, there is an opportunity for empowerment. I slowly crawled out of the back bottom bunk that sat practically on the floor reflecting where I was, bottom of the bottom. I was directed by what I would call the ladies that may have been there for a while as they seemed to direct the new people. I thought they were helpful and certainly came to see everyone as people who were also caught up in a judicial system that resulted in serving unnecessary time. People in jail are not bad people, they are people who made mistakes and while trying to get everything headed in the right direction keep getting placed back into a not so serving system. A few questions arose. Like, how is it ok or even humane to keep people in a jail with no reform. Why did I have to ask more than ten times to get access to something like a book or bible and get denied because I asked to many times. Do people in jail get access to daylight, in this oh so dark room? How long do they stay in this room? Why did it take over five hours to get booked and why did I have to remain in cuffs on a chair for hours? Why was I subject to radiation when getting booked into jail? Why did I have to get asked the same questions by the officer and then again by the nurse? And why could I not call anyone unless I gave my voice to a global AI for reorganization? How much does it cost taxpayers to keep me in jail?

Determined to bring attention to the flaws in the New Mexico judicial system, I decided to use my experience as a catalyst for change.

My experience exposed the impracticality of a system that denies individuals the right to post bail until they have seen a judge or probation officer. It highlighted the lack of communication and notification, leaving people unaware of their legal obligations until it is too late.

Recommendations for reforming the system.

1.

Improving communication channels, ensuring timely notifications, and allowing individuals like me to post bail before facing a judge on minor incidents like such. This would not only protect the rights of citizens but also streamline the judicial process.

2.

Software made for the gathering data and

filtering out the charges by rank.

Communication with systems could help

gather valuable data and help people in the

community resolve social economic issues

and other identifying issues.

There is a clear need for more of our state

funds to be allocated to our software systems.

Those roads are a key to better drive in our

systems.

As a call to action, let's vow to advocate for change, shedding light on the shortcomings of the New Mexico judicial system. My journey from terror to empowerment became a beacon of resilience, it is my hope to inspire others to stand against injustice and fight for a fair compassionate legal system.

The New Mexico Courts website can be found by conducting an online search or by visiting the following URL:

New Mexico Courts Official Website

Please note that specific information regarding bail procedures and related legal matters may be available within the relevant sections of the website or by contacting the appropriate or legal authority in New Mexico.

Review the current law that affected me and so many and let's reform it to be better serving of the people.

How do you propose an amendment to a law?

Proposing an amendment to a law involves a specific process, and if can vary depending on the jurisdiction (local, state, or federal) Here is a general guide that you can follow:

1. Research the Current Law:

    - Understand the existing law that you want to amend. Identify the specific section or language you believe needs modifications.

2. **Draft the Amendment:**

- **Clearly articulate the changes you propose. Be specific and precise in your language. If possible, seek legal advice to ensure your proposed amendment is legally sound.**

3. **Identify a Sponsor:**

- **Find a legislator who is willing to sponsor your proposed amendment. This person will introduce the amendment to the legislative body.**

4. Contact Your legislators:

- Research out your local
  representatives and senators to
  discuss your proposed
  amendment. Explain why you
  believe the change is necessary
  and how it will benefit the
  community or address and issue.

5. Build Support:

- Garner support from individuals,
  organizations, or advocacy groups
  that share our perspective. A well-
  supported amendment is more
  likely to gain traction.

6. **Present to Committees:**

    - **If the legislative process involves committees, present your proposed amendment to the relevant committees. Be prepared to answer questions and provide additional information.**

7. **Publicize Your Cause:**

    - **Use various channels to publicize your cause, including social media, community meetings, and local news outlets. Building public awareness and support can influence the legislative process.**

8. Lobbying:

- Consider engaging in lobbying
  efforts to promote your proposed
  amendment. This may involve
  meeting with legislators, attending
  hearings and providing additional
  information.

9. Legislative Approval:

- If your proposed amendment gains
  support, it will go through the
  legislative process, including
  debates, votes, and committee
  reviews. If it passes, it may be sent
  to the executive branch for
  approval, depending on the
  legislative structure.

10.   Implementations:

- Once the amendment is approved, it becomes part of the law. Ensure that any necessary agencies or entities are aware of the changes and implement them accordingly.

Keep in mind that the specific procedures and requirements for proposing amendments can vary, so it's essential to familiarize yourself with the legislative process in your jurisdiction. Additionally, consulting with legal experts or experienced advocates can provide valuable insight and guidance.

<u>Let's keep our right to make America Great and come together with our experiences to continue to evolve and make our governs serve us.</u>

Buckle up

This ride is starting.

Current New Mexico Legislators

Name	Phone	Email

Take Action: Notes:

23

Take Action: Notes:

Take Action: Notes:

25

Take Action: Notes:

Key Contact organizations?

Take Action: Notes:

Take Action: Notes:

29

Take Action: Notes:

30